For Elias, Adeline, and Ezra

Text copyright © 2022 by Matthew Paul Turner
Illustrations copyright © 2022 by Estrella Bascuñan

Published in the United States by Convergent Books,
an imprint of Random House, a division of
Penguin Random House LLC, New York.

CONVERGENT BOOKS is a registered trademark
and its C colophon is a trademark
of Penguin Random House LLC.

ISBN 978-0-593-23473-0
Ebook ISBN 978-0-593-23474-7

The Library of Congress catalog record is
available at https://lccn.loc.gov/2021013936.

Printed in China

convergentbooks.com

10 9 8 7 6 5 4 3 2 1

First Edition

Book and cover design by Ashley Tucker and Sonia Persad
Cover illustrations by Estrella Bascuñan

I AM GOD'S DREAM

Matthew Paul Turner

CONVERGENT

Illustrated by
Estrella Bascuñan

I am God's dream!
I'm a human **sunbeam.**

Watch me light up a room
with my confident gleam.

I'm **playful** and **brave.**
I'm a one-kid parade.

I will be who I am
'cause I'm **wonderfully made.**

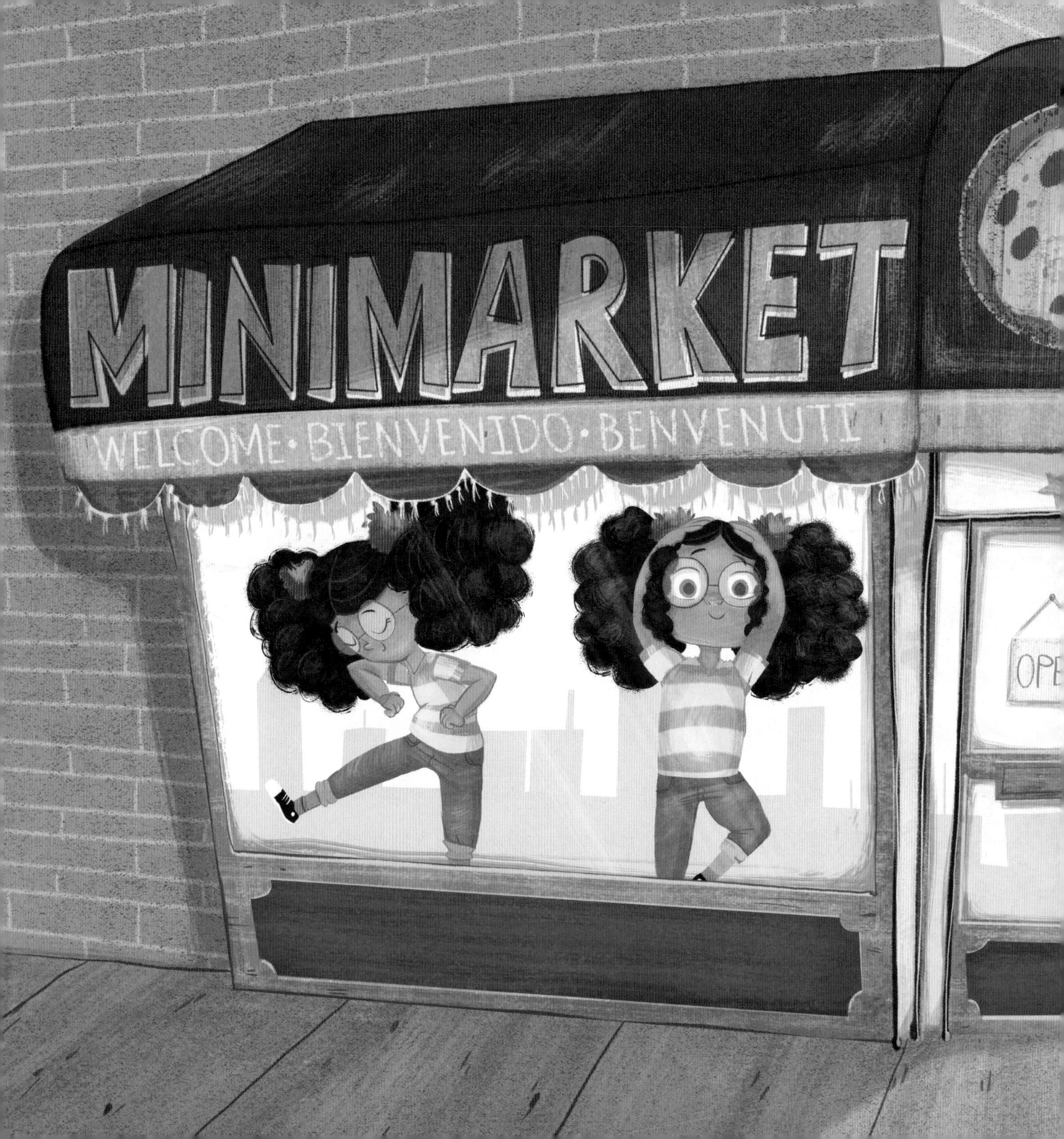
MINIMARKET
WELCOME • BIENVENIDO • BENVENUTI
OPE

When I look in the mirror,
I love who I see.
I like how I look
when I'm staring at me—

my face and my skin
and my big goofy grin.
I love how I feel
when I **wiggle** and **spin.**

I love how my hair
has a **mind** of its own,
how it does what it wants
despite gel and a comb.

And I love how my eyes
GROW BIG and get wide
when I'm startled or mad
or excited inside.

I **love** my mouth and my nose.

I even **love** my elbows.

I think I look good when I'm striking this pose.

I love how my belly can **jiggle** around
when I dance or I skip
or I hang upside down.

With my hands and my feet,
I can make my own beat
and **move to the rhythm** God put inside me.

This body is mine!
And I'll treat it so kind.
I'll **value** and love
what I know God designed.

'Cause God made me **me,**
and one day you'll see
the dream that God's dreaming—
that's who I will be.

I am God's light.
Like a spark, I **IGNITE**.
Loved just as I am,
I'm a star in God's sight.

I'm delightful
and smart.
I am God's
work of art.

I will live
every moment
with **all of my heart.**

When I look in the mirror, I think of what's true:
that God **loves** me and wants me to **love** myself too.

That I was made to be ***free!***
And the brilliance you see?
That's the **light** that exists
on the inside of me.

So I love who I am,
the me deep inside—
so **quirky** and curious,
creative and **kind**.

DRAMATIC! And clever.
But neat? Hardly ever.

I'm messy and clumsy,
yet God calls me **a treasure!**

I love the me who tells jokes
and then **snorts** when I **laugh**.
And the me who protests
every shower and bath.

My obnoxious side,
how I get tongue tied,
and the me who tries hard
and **still** fails sometimes.

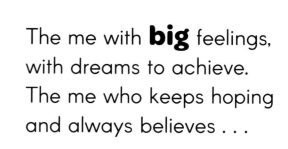

The me with **big** feelings,
with dreams to achieve.
The me who keeps hoping
and always believes . . .

that God's writing my story,
something **good** and not boring,

that I'm here for a **purpose** and each day's worth exploring!

So I'll use all my gifts, every skill, all my **talent**
to bring beauty, to empower, to resist, and to challenge.

Because all of my being has value and meaning,
and I believe in my heart that God never stops dreaming.

'Cause God made me *me* and **bright** as can be—
and the brilliance I bring will be hard to unsee.

I am God's child. I'm silly and **WILD.**
I'm one of the billions of reasons God smiles.

I'm courageous and true. I'm a dream God pursues.
You might be surprised what God knows I can do!

When I look in the mirror, I can see what God sees,

the human I know that God made me to be.

I see my hands and my feet;
I feel my heart make its **beat**.

And in all that I am,
I glimpse God within me.

When I smile, when I cry,
every time that I'm shy.
When I fall over **laughing**
or dare to ask why.
When I'm hopeful or scared,
when I don't feel prepared,
when you ask who I am
and **bravely** I share.

When I look at my friends
and I see God in them,
when I fall or I fail
and I get up and try again.
When I'm happy,
when I grieve,
when I struggle to believe.
Every moment, every day, *in me*,
God lives and breathes!

So I'll love and be kind
and in hope remain grounded.
I'll fight the good fight
and with faith move a mountain.
I'll find **joy** and make **peace**
and help justice increase.
This fire in me I'll let God help unleash.

I'll do all I can to build and to mend,
to love what God loves, to heal and transcend.
I'll use all I am to love stranger and friend
and try to help others see
God's dreams for **them.**

'Cause to God I'm divine,
full of **wonder** and **shine**.
I will live every day
with all **heart**, **soul**, and **mind**.

'Cause God made me *me*,
and I can't wait to see
the dream that God dreams,
the dream God calls . . . *me!*